Yanks in WWI

Americans in the Trenches

Sean Price

Chicago, Illinois

RAINTREE

TO ORDER:

☎ Phone Customer Service **888-454-2279**

💻 Visit **www.heinemannraintree.com** to browse our catalog and order online.

Editorial: Adam Miller
Design: Ryan Frieson, Kimberly R. Miracle, and Betsy Wernert
Photo Research: Tracy Cummins
Production: Victoria Fitzgerald

Originated by DOT Gradation Ltd.
Printed and bound by Leo Paper Group.

ISBN-13: 978-1-4109-3110-8 (hc)
ISBN-10: 1-4109-3110-2 (hc)
ISBN-13: 978-1-4109-3119-1 (pb)
ISBN-10: 1-4109-3119-6 (pb)

13 12 11 10 09
10 9 8 7 6 5 4 3 2 1

Library of Congress Cataloging-in-Publication Data
Price, Sean.
  Yanks in World War I : Americans in the trenches / Sean Price.
      p. cm. -- (American history through primary sources)
   Includes bibliographical references and index.
ISBN 978-1-4109-3110-8 (hc) --
ISBN 978-1-4109-3119-1 (pb)1. World War, 1914-1918--United States--Juvenile literature. 2. World War, 1914-1918--United States--Sources--Juvenile literature. 3. United States. Army--Military life--History--20th century--Juvenile literature. 4. United States. Army--Military life--History--20th century--Sources--Juvenile literature. I. Title. II. Title: Yanks in World War One. III. Title: Yanks in World War 1.

D570.P75 2008
940.4'0973--dc22
                                            2008011288

Acknowledgments
The author and publisher are grateful to the following for permission to reproduced copyright material: ©The Art Archive **p. 23** (Culver Pictures); ©Associaated Press **pp. 14, 27, 29**; ©Corbis **pp. 16, 25-T, 25-B** (Bettmann), **19** (Hulton-Deutsch Collection); ©Getty Images **pp. 4, 5** (Popperfoto), **7** (Topical Press Agency/Stringer), **17** (Time & Life Pictures), **18** (Getty Images); ©The Granger Collection **pp. 6, 8, 15**; ©Library of Congress **pp. 9-B, 10, 11-B, 24** (Prints and Photographs Division), **11-T** (Serials and Government Publications Division); ©National Archives at College Park **pp. 9-T, 12, 13, 20, 21, 28**.

Cover image of an American soldier writing a letter in the trenches, December 17, 1917, used with permission of ©Corbis/Bettmann.

The publishers would like to thank Nancy Harris for her assistance in the preparation of this book.

Contents

The War Begins

World War I began with two murders. A gunman killed the Archduke Franz Ferdinand and his wife. Ferdinand was from the country of Austria-Hungary. He was the son of that country's top leader. The archduke was supposed to become top leader, too.

World War I started with the shooting of Archduke Franz Ferdinand.

Most countries in Europe split into two groups. On one side were the **Allies**. On the other were the **Central Powers**.

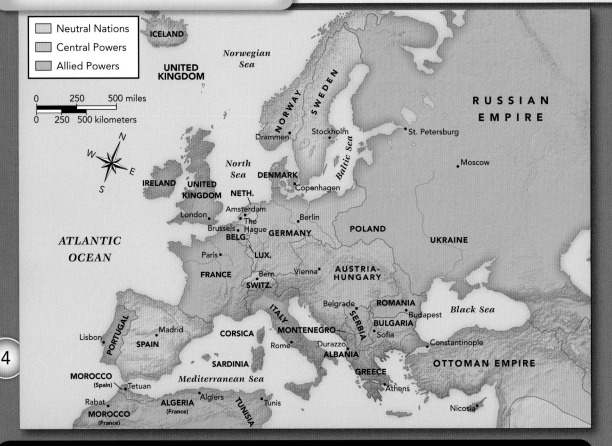

Neutral Nations	
Central Powers	
Allied Powers	

0   250   500 miles
0   250   500 kilometers

ICELAND

Norwegian Sea

UNITED KINGDOM

NORWAY SWEDEN

RUSSIAN EMPIRE

Drammen · Stockholm · St. Petersburg

Baltic Sea

North Sea

IRELAND UNITED KINGDOM

DENMARK
· Copenhagen

· Moscow

NETH.

Amsterdam

London · · The Hague · Berlin

Brussels · BELG. GERMANY POLAND UKRAINE

ATLANTIC OCEAN

Paris · LUX.

FRANCE · Bern Vienna · AUSTRIA-HUNGARY

SWITZ.

Belgrade · ROMANIA Black Sea
· Budapest

ITALY MONTENEGRO SERBIA BULGARIA
· Sofia

PORTUGAL · Madrid CORSICA Durazzo · · Constantinople

Lisbon · SPAIN Rome · ALBANIA

SARDINIA GREECE OTTOMAN EMPIRE

MOROCCO (Spain) Mediterranean Sea · Athens

· Tetuan

Rabat · ALGERIA (France) · Algiers · Tunis · Nicosia

MOROCCO (France) TUNISIA

Central Powers   countries led by Germany, Austria-Hungary, and Turkey

Men all over Europe joined armies. Most trained very quickly to become soldiers. Then they were sent to fight.

Ferdinand and his wife were killed in their car. They were driving in a city called Sarajevo (*sar-ah-YEH-voh*). It was in Austria-Hungary. The gunman was Gavrillo Princip (*gahv-REEL-oh PREEN-szeep*). He was from Serbia (see the map). Serbia was a small country. It is next to Austria-Hungary. Princip believed that Serbs living in Austria-Hungary were not free. He wanted to free them. He believed shooting Ferdinand and his wife would do this.

Instead, Princip's act started a war. At first, the war was between Serbia and Austria-Hungary. But both countries called on others to take a side. Many more countries joined the conflict. Most of them were in Europe. People soon called it "the Great War." Today, we call it World War I.

"All the News That's Fit to Print."

The New York Times.

EXTRA
5:30 A. M.

VOL. LXIV...NO. 20,923.

NEW YORK, SATURDAY, MAY 8, 1915.—TWENTY-FOUR PAGES.

ONE CENT In Greater New York, Jersey City and Newark. Elsewhere TWO CENTS.

LUSITANIA SUNK BY A SUBMARINE, PROBABLY 1,260 DEAD; TWICE TORPEDOED OFF IRISH COAST; SINKS IN 15 MINUTES; CAPT. TURNER SAVED, FROHMAN AND VANDERBILT MISSING; WASHINGTON BELIEVES THAT A GRAVE CRISIS IS AT HAND

SHOCKS THE PRESIDENT

Washington Deeply Stirred by the Loss of American Lives.

BULLETINS AT WHITE HOUSE

Wilson Reads Them Closely, but Is Silent on the Nation's Course.

HINTS OF CONGRESS CALL

Loss of Lusitania Recalls Firm Tone of Our First Warning to Germany.

CAPITAL FULL OF RUMORS

Reports That Liner Was to be Sunk Were Heard Before Actual News Came.

SOME DEAD TAKEN ASHORE

Several Hundred Survivors at Queenstown and Kinsale.

STEWARD TELLS OF DISASTER

One Torpedo Crashes Into the Doomed Liner's Bow, Another Into the Engine Room.

SHIP LISTS OVER TO PORT

Makes It Impossible to Lower Many Boats, So Hundreds Must Have Gone Down.

ATTACKED IN BROAD DAY

Passengers at Luncheon—Warning Had Been Given by Germans Before the Ship Left New York.

Only 650 Were Saved

> Americans were neutral in the war. But they became angry at Germany. A German submarine sank this ship.

Americans join the fight

Europe's most powerful countries joined the war. On one side there were England, France, and Russia. These countries sided with Serbia. They were called "the **Allies**." On the other side, there were Germany, Austria-Hungary, and Turkey. These countries were called "the **Central Powers**."

The United States did not join the war at first. It stayed **neutral**. It did not pick a side. Most Americans did not want to fight in a war overseas. That feeling began to change in 1915. A ship called the *Lusitania* was sunk. It was sunk by a German **submarine**. A submarine is a ship that can travel under water. More than 120 Americans died in the sinking.

Many who died on the *Lusitania* were buried in mass graves. Photos like this one shocked people around the world.

Then in 1917, Germany sent a message to the country of Mexico. The Germans asked Mexico to attack the United States. Mexico refused. But Americans found out about this message. On April 6, 1917, the United States joined the war. Americans were on the side of the Allies.

Americans Go "Over There"

Americans felt they were fighting for a good cause. The **Central Powers** were not free countries. Americans believed that the war would free people in those countries.

Patriotic songs became very popular. They make people feel good about their country. Perhaps the most popular was "Over There." It was by George M. Cohan. Its chorus went like this:

The song "Over There" summed up how Americans felt about the war.

Over there, over there

Send the word, send the word over there

That the **Yanks** (Americans) are coming, the Yanks are coming,

The drums rum-tumming everywhere

So prepare, say a prayer

Send the word, send the word to beware

We'll be over, we're coming over,

And we won't come back till it's over over there.

These American soldiers are in France. They are heading to the battle line.

Yanks and Doughboys

People came up with nicknames for U.S. soldiers. Some called U.S. soldiers Yanks. This was short for Yankee. U.S. soldiers were also called "**Doughboys**." There are many ideas about where this name came from. But no one is certain which idea is true.

Doughboys mainly fought in France. A soldier's life was hard and full of danger.

Joining up

The United States was not ready to go to war. Its army was very small. Posters like this one urged men to **volunteer**. That meant they joined the army or navy willingly. Many men did volunteer. But most men were **drafted**. That meant they were ordered to join the army or navy by the **government**. The government makes the country's rules.

The U.S. soldiers were young men. Most were between 21 and 23 years old. Some were as young as 17. Most had never been far from home. Few had fired a gun. They had to be trained to fight.

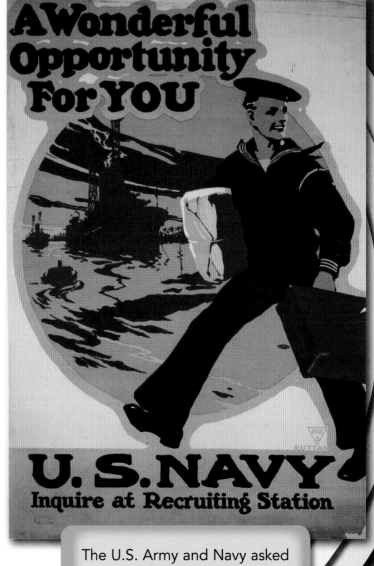

A Wonderful Opportunity For YOU

U.S. NAVY
Inquire at Recruiting Station

The U.S. Army and Navy asked men to volunteer. Both needed many men to fight.

OVERSEA CAP

PONCHO AND
BLANKET

BAYONET

STEEL HELMET

CARTRIDGE
BELT

KNAPSACK

WATER BOTTLE

HAVERSACK

FIRST AID
PACKAGE

GAS
MASK

ENTRENCHING
TOOL

SPRINGFIELD
RIFLE

PUTTEES
(SPIRAL)

PUTTEES
(SPIRAL)

FRONT AND BACK VIEW OF AN AMERICAN INFANTRYMAN, COMPLETELY
EQUIPPED FROM HEAD TO FOOT AND READY FOR ACTION.

ALL MEMBERS OF THE INFANTRY DIVISIONS OF THE AMERICAN NATIONAL ARMY WERE REQUIRED
TO UNDERGO AN ARDUOUS TRAINING IN BAYONET WORK. MASKS AND PADDED COATS PROTECTED
FROM INJURY.

SIGHTING A RIFLE IN TRAINING AT PLATTSBURG WHERE THOUSANDS OF OFFICERS FOR THE
RAPIDLY GROWING AMERICAN ARMY WERE QUICKLY AND EFFICIENTLY DEVELOPED.

Men trained hard to become soldiers. They had to carry everything they needed with them. They also had to be able to shoot and fight quickly.

PERSHING'S CRUSADERS

AUSPICES OF THE
UNITED STATES GOVERNMENT
·THE FIRST OFFICIAL AMERICAN WAR PICTURE·
TAKEN BY U.S. SIGNAL CORPS AND NAVY PHOTOGRAPHERS

Their training took only a few weeks. It was tough. The men had to exercise a lot. Soldiers had to be strong in order to fight. Soldiers also learned to obey officers. **Officers** were the people who made important decisions. The top officer was General John J. Pershing. He led all the U.S. soldiers who fought in the war.

11

Americans were led by General John J. Pershing. Pershing became a hero in America.

The home front

Young men went off to fight the war. But people were needed to do their jobs at home.

Young women stepped in to fill their place. This seemed strange at the time. Most women did not work. They stayed at home. They focused on cleaning and taking care of children. But during the war women worked in **factories**. That is a business that makes things. Women did jobs that were seen as "male." Many women liked this work. It gave them more money. It made them feel independent.

Women worked in factories. They made rifles, bombs, and planes. This work could be very dangerous.

Blacks also took many factory jobs. Most blacks lived in the southern states. But they faced terrible hatred there from whites. Most factories were in the north. People were needed to fill factory jobs. Newspapers urged blacks to take these jobs. Many blacks headed north to do that. They went north to get a better life. This period is called the Great **Migration**. A migration is a huge movement of many people.

Before the war, blacks did not often work with whites. This changed during the war. Blacks and whites were hired and worked together.

migration huge movement of people

In the Trenches

Soldiers in World War I fought in **trenches**. These were big ditches.

Soldiers dug trenches. Trenches helped protect them from bullets and bombs. But life in the trenches was hard. The enemy trenches were always close by. It was easy for enemy soldiers to shoot at American trenches. The area between the trenches was called "No Man's Land." It was called that because no man could stay alive for long there. He would be shot.

This American soldier is about to throw a small bomb called a grenade. He is throwing it into No Man's Land.

trench   ditch in the ground. It allows soldiers to hide from enemy fire.

Soldiers could not leave the trenches. If they did, they would be shot. They had to do everything in the trenches.

Trenches became muddy in the rain. Men had to sleep in holes in the sides of the trenches. Trenches smelled bad as well. Men had few places to go to the bathroom. Dead bodies also smell bad. So the smell of death was everywhere.

Unwelcome guests

Rats were common in the trenches. They were attracted by the bad smells. Sometimes rats ran across soldiers while they slept. Lice were also a problem. Lice are small bugs. They suck blood. They cause terrible itching.

15

Gas attacks often blinded soldiers. Some got their vision back. Others were blinded for life.

Poison gas

World War I saw the use of terrible new weapons. One of the worst was poison gas. Gas was first used by the Germans in 1915. But **Allies** soon used it, too.

Soldiers hated gas. It could quickly destroy the lungs. Soldiers could not breathe. Gas also damaged eyes. Many soldiers were blinded for life.

Soldiers wore gas masks. These helped them breathe during a gas attack. But gas could still hurt and kill. Gas was supposed to help end the war quickly. Instead, it just made life harder for soldiers.

New weapons of war

Gas was not the only new weapon. Soldiers had to fight against new machines like tanks and airplanes. These and other weapons were used widely for the first time. They made World War I more terrible than past wars. Here are some of the new items that were first used in World War I.

- Airplane
- Barbed Wire
- Flamethrower
- Machine Gun
- Poison Gas
- Submarine
- Tank

These soldiers are wearing gas masks. They are expecting a poison gas attack.

Over the top

Soldiers lived in constant danger. The most dangerous thing they did was go "over the top." That meant they went into No Man's Land. They attacked the enemy **trenches**.

No Man's Land was a confusing place. It was full of holes where bombs had gone off. After a rain the ground was muddy. The holes were full of dirty water. Soldiers had to run across this ground. They tried to avoid bullets and bombs. But many men were wounded or killed going "over the top."

Soldiers who went "over the top" often died or were wounded. They had no protection against enemy fire.

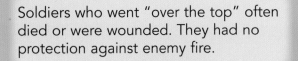

Many nurses worked close to the fighting. They had to work in the trenches to be protected from enemy fire.

Nursing the wounded

Women were not allowed to fight. But many women worked as nurses. They treated wounded soldiers. This was hard work. A lot of doctors and nurses worked close to the fighting. Bombs often went off around them while they worked. Fighting was not the only danger. Many soldiers became sick. A type of flu killed many people. It killed more people than died in all the war's fighting.

Harlem Hellfighters

Black Americans served in World War I. But they were not allowed to serve with whites. They served in all-black **units** (groups of soldiers). Most black units worked as laborers. They loaded and unloaded ships. They drove trucks. They carried heavy equipment.

The Harlem Hellfighters fought hard. All of these soldiers won medals for bravery.

Lt. Jim Europe's band

Black units brought their own music to France. That music was called **jazz**. Jazz was a new type of music created by blacks. People in France liked it. Lt. Jim Europe was a black U.S. soldier. He led a military band. His band played jazz a lot. Europe's band was a big hit. It helped spread jazz worldwide.

Only four black units were allowed to fight. They had to fight as part of the French Army. They wore French uniforms. They fought with white French soldiers. These black soldiers showed great bravery. They won many medals. The French admired these soldiers. The French treated blacks better than white Americans did. The most famous black unit was the Harlem Hellfighters. Harlem is in New York City. Mostly black people lived there.

21

Alvin York

The biggest American hero of the war was Alvin York. York did not want to fight in the war at first. He did not believe in killing. His officers talked to him. They showed him that fighting was needed sometimes.

York turned out to be a good soldier. In 1918, his unit was under attack. German machine guns were killing men all around him. Only York and a few other men were still unhurt. York led those men. Together, they killed 25 Germans. They stopped 35 German machine guns. They also captured 132 prisoners.

York was given many medals. One was the **Medal of Honor**. It is the highest award a U.S. soldier can receive. A soldier must do something very brave to win it.

Dog tags

Like all soldiers, York had **dog tags**. These were metal disks that a soldier wore around his neck. They let people know who he was if he was hurt or killed.

dog tag   metal disk that identifies a soldier

Alvin York became one of the
war's biggest heroes. He won
the Medal of Honor for bravery.

Fighting boredom

Life in the **trenches** was not all action. Soldiers sat around a lot. They had nothing to do. They became very bored.

Soldiers played games to break the boredom. The games they played included chess and checkers. Soldiers also liked to write letters. Often they sent home postcards. Postcards had pictures on one side. They had space to write on the other. Many postcards showed photos of soldiers. Other postcards showed battlefields where men fought. Some even showed dead bodies.

Soldiers liked to read. They read books and magazines. The army made a newspaper for soldiers. It was called *The Stars and Stripes*. Soldiers liked its cartoons and articles.

The Stars and Stripes was a newspaper written for soldiers and sailors.

Aid and comfort

Many groups tried to help soldiers. One of them was the Young Men's Christian Association, or YMCA. They gave soldiers food like sandwiches and hot chocolate. They also put on shows to entertain the troops. Soldiers were far from home. These things helped soldiers feel better.

Soldiers liked to get letters from home. They also liked to write them whenever they had a chance.

The Final Shots

World War I ended on November 11, 1918. The last shots were fired just before 11 a.m. Both sides kept firing their guns until the last minute. Many people died just before the war ended.

The United States helped to end the war. Americans entered the war in 1917. Other countries had been fighting for three years. These countries were running out of men. They were running out of money. But the United States still had plenty of men and money. Germany could not keep fighting. The other **Central Powers** could not keep fighting either.

In 1919, the two sides signed a peace **treaty** (agreement). It was supposed to stop all fighting. World War I was supposed to be the "war to end all wars." But that did not happen. The peace treaty was unfair to Germany. Germans became angry about this. In 1939, Germany started World War II. That war was even more terrible than World War I.

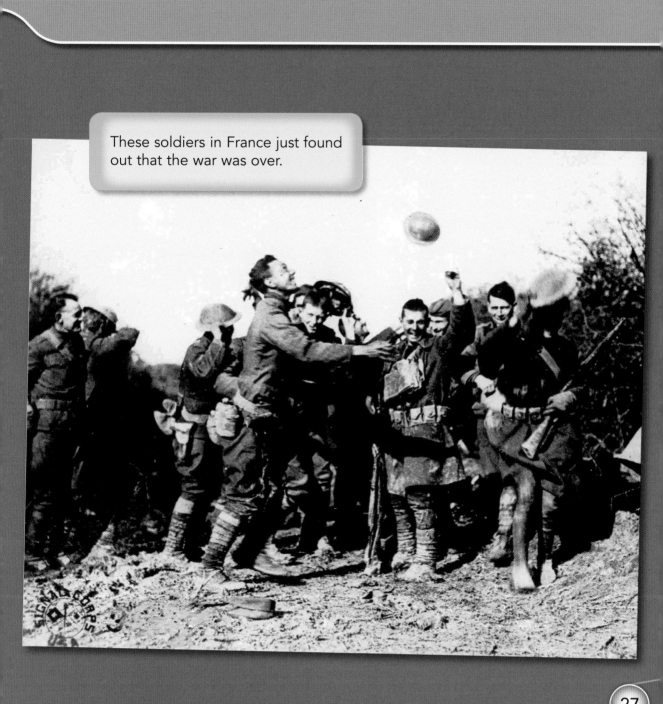

These soldiers in France just found out that the war was over.

Coming home

U.S. soldiers joyfully returned home in 1918 and 1919. Many of them were greeted by parades. They marched before hometown crowds. Many friends and family came to see them. They were glad that the soldiers were home.

Many men had died in the war. Others were badly hurt. Some had lost legs or arms. These soldiers could not march in parades. People remembered them though. Americans were very proud of them.

People were very happy that the war was over. People crowded the streets to celebrate.

Many soldiers returned to normal life. They returned to their jobs. They got married and had kids. But some had a hard time after the war. They had seen terrible things in combat. They could not forget them. Some were bothered by nightmares.

The war caused many hardships. Yet many men remembered good things about it. They had lived in danger with other men. They had shared the hardships together. That made these men very close to one another. They felt like brothers.

Both big cities and small towns held parades to welcome back returning soldiers and sailors. Here, General John J. Pershing watches a parade in New York City.

Glossary

Allies countries led by Great Britain, France, and Russia. The United States later joined the Allies.

Central Powers countries led by Germany, Austria-Hungary, and Turkey

dog tag metal disk that identifies a soldier

Doughboy nickname for any U.S. solider

drafted ordered to do something by the government

factory place where things are made

government group of people who run a country

jazz type of music created by black Americans

Medal of Honor the highest award a U.S. soldier can receive

migration huge movement of people

neutral refusing to pick a side

officers people who make the important decisions in wars

patriotic song song that makes people feel good about their country

submarine ship that moves under water

treaty agreement to end a war

trench ditch in the ground. It allows soldiers to hide from enemy fire.

unit group of soldiers

volunteer someone who does something willingly

Yank nickname for any U.S. soldier

Want to Know More?

Books to read

Adams, Simon. *Eyewitness: World War I*. New York: Dorling Kindersley, 2004.

Price, Sean. *In the Trenches: World War I*. New York: Harcourt, 2007.

Websites

http://london.iwm.org.uk/server/show/nav.00p001
Find out about World War I through first-hand sources at London's Imperial War Museum.

http://memory.loc.gov/ammem/collections/rotogravures/rotogal2.html
These Library of Congress photos show what life was like during the war.

Places to visit

The National World War One Museum
100 W. 26th Street • Kansas City, MO 64108-4616 • 816-784-1918
http://www.info@nwwone.org

Read *The Roaring Twenties: America Has Fun* to find out what life was like in America after World War I.

Read *The Art of War: Posters of World War II* to find out about America's role in the next World War.

Index